Colors

White

Nancy Harris

Heinemann Library
Chicago, Illinois

HEINEMANN-RAINTREE

TO ORDER:
☎ Call Customer Service (Toll-Free) **1-888-454-2279**
💻 Visit **heinemannraintree.com** to browse our catalog and order online.

Editorial: Rebecca Rissman
Design: Kimberly R. Miracle and Joanna Hinton-Malivoire
Photo Research: Tracy Cummins and Tracey Engel
Production: Duncan Gilbert

Originated by Dot
Printed and bound by South China Printing Company
The paper used to print this book comes from sustainable resources.

ISBN-13: 978-1-4329-1595-7 (hc)
ISBN-10: 1-4329-1595-9 (hc)
ISBN-13: 978-1-4329-1605-3 (pb)
ISBN-10: 1-4329-1605-X (pb)

12 11 10 09 08
10 9 8 7 6 5 4 3 2 1

**Library of Congress
Cataloging-in-Publication Data**
Harris, Nancy, 1956-
White / Nancy Harris.
    p. cm. -- (Colors)   6969
Includes bibliographical references and index.
ISBN 978-1-4329-1595-7 (hc) -- ISBN 978-1-4329-1605-3 (pb)
1. White--Juvenile literature. 2. Color--Juvenile literature. I. Title.
QC495.5.H378 2008
535.6--dc22

2008005613

Acknowledgments
The author and publisher are grateful to the following for permission to reproduce copyright material: ©Alamy **p. 6** (John Glover); ©CORBIS **pp. 14, 23a** (Frank Lane Picture Agency/Chris Mattison); ©Dreamstime.com **p. 4** Top Center (Basslinegfx); ©istockphoto **pp. 5** Bottom Left (Moritz von Hacht), **5** Top Right (Viktor Neimanis), **16, 22b** (Dmitry Deshevykh); ©photos.com **pp. 5** Bottom Center, **12, 19;** ©Shutterstock **pp. 4** Bottom Center (Gnuskin Petr), **4** Bottom Left (Maceofoto), **4** Bottom Right (Keith Levit), **4** Top Left, **10, 22a** (Elena Elisseeva), **4** Top Right (Humberto Ortega), **5** Bottom Right, **20, 22d, 23b** (Susan Gottberg), **5** Top Center (Philip Lange), **5** Top Left, **18, 22c** (fat_fa_tin), **7** (coko), **8** (Jean-Louis Vosgien), **9** (Goodmood photos), **11** (Joshua Haviv), **13** (beltsazar), **15** (Peter Hansen), **17** (Joe Gough), **21** (Liz Van Steenburgh).

Cover photograph reproduced with permission of ©Getty Images/ Digital Vision/Tom Brakefield.

Back cover photograph reproduced with permission of ©Shutterstock/ Susan Gottberg.

The publishers would like to thank Nancy Harris for her assistance in the preparation of this book.

Every effort has been made to contact copyright holders of any material reproduced in this book. Any omissions will be rectified in subsequent printings if notice is given to the publisher.

Contents

White

Are all plants white?

Are all animals white?

Are all rocks white?

Are all soils white?

Plants

Some leaves are white.

Some leaves are not white.

Some stems are white.

Some stems are not white.

Some flowers are white.

Some flowers are not white.

Animals

Some feathers are white.

Some feathers are not white.

Some scales are white.

Some scales are not white.

Some fur is white.

Some fur is not white.

Rocks

Some rocks are white.

Some rocks are not white.

Soil

Some soil is white.

Some soil is not white.

What Have You Learned?

Some plants are white.

Some animals are white.

Some rocks are white.

Some soils are white.

Picture Glossary

scale small plate that covers the body of some animals

soil mix of small rocks and dead plants. Plants grow in soil.

Content Vocabulary for Teachers

body covering outer layer, such as skin or scales, that protects an animal

color depends on the light that an object reflects or absorbs

Index

Note to Parents and Teachers

Before reading:
Talk with children about colors. Explain that there are many different colors, and that each color has a name. Use a color wheel or other simple color chart to point to name each color. Then, ask children to make a list of the colors they can see. After they have completed their list, ask children to share their results.

After reading:
Take children on a nature or neighborhood walk. Ask them to make a list of every white object they see on their walk. Encourage them to look for little things, such as pebbles, and big things, such as cars or buildings. After the walk, ask children to group the objects in their list according to size.

JAN   2010